WOMEN'S RIGHTS AND NOTHING LESS
The Story of Elizabeth Cady Stanton

WOMEN'S RIGHTS AND NOTHING LESS
The Story of Elizabeth Cady Stanton

Lisa Frederiksen Bohannon

MORGAN
REYNOLDS
Incorporated

Greensboro

WOMEN'S RIGHTS AND NOTHING LESS
THE STORY OF ELIZABETH CADY STANTON

Copyright © 2001 by Lisa Frederiksen Bohannon

Picture credits: Unless otherwise noted, photographs are courtesy of The Library
of Congress.

Library of Congress Cataloging-in-Publication Division

Bohannon, Lisa Frederiksen.
    Women's rights and nothing less : the story of Elizabeth Cady Stanton / Lisa
Frederiksen Bohannon.
      p. cm.
    Includes bibliographical references and index.
    ISBN 1-883846-66-8 (lib. bdg.)
      1. Stanton, Elizabeth Cady, 1815-1902--Juvenile literature. 2. Feminists United
States--Biography--Juvenile literature. 3. Women's rights--United States--History--19th
century--Juvenile literature. I. Title. II. Series.

HQ1413.S67 B65 2000
305.42'092--dc21
[B]

                                                              00-025565

Printed in the United States of America
First Edition

For my daughters,
Jessica Erin and Kathryn Marie Scott,
with love.

Contents

Elizabeth Cady Stanton
(*From the archives of the Seneca Falls Historical Society.*)

Chapter One

Johnstown, New York

When Elizabeth Cady was eleven years old, her older brother Eleazer died. Eleazar had just graduated from Union College in Schenectady, New York, and had been the pride of the Cady family. He was the fourth of the Cady children to die.

Soon after Eleazer's death, Elizabeth found her pale and almost immovable father in the darkened parlor, sitting next to the casket. All the mirrors and pictures were draped in white. Her father took no notice of Elizabeth as she climbed upon his knee. His arm mechanically circled her waist. For a long time he said nothing, nor did she as she rested her head against his chest. Finally, with great sadness, her father sighed, "Oh, my daughter, I wish you were a boy!" Throwing her arms around his neck, she replied, "I will try to be all my brother was." There and then, Elizabeth decided that she would do whatever it took to be as much like a boy as she possibly could. She was not yet ready to ask herself the question: "Why is being a girl not good enough?"

Before her brother's death, Elizabeth had lived a happy childhood in a wealthy, conservative family. She was born on November 12, 1815, in Johnstown, New York. Elizabeth's mother, Margaret Livingston Cady, was "a tall, queenly looking woman, who was courageous, self-reliant and at her ease under all circumstances and in all places." Mrs. Cady gave birth to eleven children but only five survived. Like most wealthy women, Mrs. Cady spent her time running the household, managing a large staff of servants, and preparing for social engagements.

Elizabeth described her father, Judge Daniel Cady, as "a man of firm character and unimpeachable integrity, and yet sensitive and modest to a painful degree." Unlike her mother, Elizabeth's father did not seem at ease in society. He preferred to be at work or at home sitting by the fireplace. Judge Cady was a highly respected lawyer in Johnstown. He was elected to the U.S. Congress the year Elizabeth was born.

Elizabeth was closest to her sister Margaret. Two years younger, Margaret was bigger—and bolder. While playing one day, Elizabeth complained about the fact that there were so many things they were not allowed to do. Margaret suggested a way to solve the problem: "Hereafter let us act as we choose, without asking." When Elizabeth pointed out that they would be punished, Margaret responded, "Suppose we are. We shall have had our fun at any rate, and that is better than to mind the everlasting 'no' and not have any fun at all."

Margaret Livingston Cady was, according to her daughter Elizabeth, a regal woman.

Nurses and servants were primarily responsible for caring for the Cady children. The nurses used strong discipline, severe punishment, and a firm Christian faith to ensure the children's obedience. The fear of eternal damnation particularly terrified Elizabeth. In her autobiography, she wrote that her "seventy years of trials, cares, anxieties, and disappointments, seemed light when balanced with the sufferings in childhood and youth from the gloom associated with everything in the name of religion, the church, the parsonage, the graveyard, and the solemn tolling of church bells." Although Elizabeth questioned why her parents and church considered so many things sinful, she was convinced that her rebelliousness was a bad trait. She believed that the devil would one day claim her. Sometimes her fears were overwhelming. She would spend the night crouched on the stairs where the hall lamp and the sound of adult voices in the parlor eased her terror.

One servant named Peter cared for Elizabeth and her two younger sisters, Catherine and Margaret. Peter kept track of the girls, making sure they were not late for school in the morning and were home in time for dinner. Elizabeth and her sisters adored Peter because he was kind and shared their curiosity for new ideas.

Peter's attitude toward religion was different than the frightening sermons on hellfire and damnation that Elizabeth heard at her church. His faith gave him comfort. This was a new perspective for Elizabeth. Peter occasionally took the younger Cady sisters to his church. The girls would sit in the "Negro's pew" with Peter instead of in the front of the church with the white people.

Elizabeth and Margaret loved to play outdoors in the winter with their siblings. They built snow statues and forts and pretended that the snow-covered woodpiles were the Swiss Alps. They also liked to play in the cellar and attic of their white, two-story, frame house. Barrels of vegetables, salt meats, apples, cider, and butter were stored in the cellar, making great hiding places. Hickory nuts, cakes of maple sugar, and all kinds of dried herbs and sweet flag were stored in the attic among old clothes. The Cady children spent hours in the attic playing dress-up, eating the sharp edges off the maple sugar cakes, cracking hickory nuts, and chewing on favorite herbs. The fact that the attic was forbidden to the children made their adventures even more exciting.

In 1826, a girl's education usually consisted of instruction that would make her a good wife and mother. Elizabeth, like her sisters, received a minimal education from Maria Yost, a spinster who taught the Cady children the "rudiments of the English language, the multiplication table, and the points of the compass." Mathematics, science, literature, or history were not necessary to run a household or care for children, people argued. Why waste time and money educating a girl. After all, wasn't a girl's brain smaller than a boy's?

After her brother's death, Elizabeth asked Reverend Simon Hosack to help make her more like a boy. Reverend Hosack taught at the Johnstown Academy. He agreed to tutor Elizabeth in Greek. She surprised the reverend with her progress, and he praised her accomplishments to Judge Cady. But her father was lost in his grief; he did not hear Reverend Hosack's praise. He worried that he did not have a male heir to his large estate who would carry on the family name. Judge Cady paced his study endlessly, and when visiting the cemetery he would "throw himself on the grave, with outstretched arms, as if to embrace his child." It saddened Elizabeth to see him so distraught and hurt her deeply that he found her so unworthy of his love.

Determined to get her father's attention, Elizabeth accepted Reverend Hosack's invitation to study Greek, Latin, and mathematics with a class of boys at the Johnstown Academy. She learned to play chess—a game considered too difficult for a girl to master—and committed herself to becoming courageous. She took riding lessons and learned to "leap a fence and ditch on horseback."

After three years of study at the Johnstown Academy, Elizabeth won second prize in a Greek contest. She was convinced that her father would now be pleased with her. She ran home to tell him and proudly showed him her prize, a Greek Testament. Judge Cady opened it and questioned her. Intrigued by her answers, he asked her more questions about her classes, the teachers, and the spectators at the contest. He seemed quite pleased with

Judge Daniel Cady refused to praise Elizabeth for her merits.

her. But instead of congratulating her, he kissed Elizabeth on the head and exclaimed with a sigh, "Ah, you should have been a boy!" Despite her great promise, Judge Cady continued to believe that a woman's place was at home.

Elizabeth was crushed because her accomplishments meant so little to her father, and she wondered why daughters were thought to be inferior to sons. She became even more determined to change her father's opinion.

Elizabeth's parents neither encouraged, nor discouraged, her education. Judge Cady seemed to not notice her sitting quietly in a corner of his law office. She read his law books and listened to his discussions with clients. It was in her father's office that she came to understand why daughters were thought to be inferior to sons—the law stated it in black and white.

Elizabeth listened as her father told women clients that they did not have a right to earn wages, spend money without their husband's permission, pursue a career, have an equal say about their children's upbringing, or go to college. By law, any property a married woman inherited from her father belonged to her husband. If her husband died, her property went to her son, and if he chose, her son could force her to leave the home. Women could not vote or hold public office. And there was even a law that allowed a husband to strike his wife as long as he did not use anything thicker than the judge's thumb.

These unfair laws upset Elizabeth, and she decided to do something about them. She took her father's law books and marked the bad laws, planning to cut them out with scissors and throw them away. Her father discovered her plan and explained to her that his law books were one set of many. If she removed these pages from his books, the laws would not change. "When you are grown up, and able to prepare a speech," he told her, "you must go down to Albany [the capital of New York] and talk to the legislators; tell them what you have seen in this office."

Elizabeth graduated from Johnstown Academy at the age of sixteen. She ranked second in her class and planned to follow the boys to Union College. Her "vexation and mortification" knew no bounds when she learned that Union College did not allow female students. (Oberlin College, in 1834, would make history by being the first university to admit women students.) "Again, I felt more keenly than ever the humiliation of the distinctions made on the ground of sex," she wrote. Elizabeth accepted the only option available to girls at that time—Troy Female Seminary.

Elizabeth thought that the founder of the school, Emma Willard, perfectly matched her "idea of a queen." Mrs. Willard was considered daring for her time. She taught the girls "delicate" subjects such as physiology. When the mothers visited the classroom, they were shocked to see a student drawing a heart, arteries, and veins on the blackboard while explaining the body's circulatory system. The mothers urged Emma Willard to cover the pages in the girls' textbooks that depicted the human body.

To her disappointment, Elizabeth was not challenged by her courses with Mrs. Willard. She claimed that she already knew just about everything taught at the Troy Female Seminary (with the exception of dancing, music, and French) because of her studies at the Johnstown Academy.

While Elizabeth was a student at Mrs. Willard's seminary, an evangelist, Reverend Charles G. Finney, began to lead daily prayer meetings at the school. Elizabeth attended them and her fear of damnation returned. "Fear of judgment seized my soul. Visions of the lost haunted my dreams. Mental anguish prostrated my health....When I returned home, I often at night roused my father from his slumbers to pray for me, lest I should be cast into the bottomless pit before morning."

Judge Cady became concerned for Elizabeth's mental well being. Believing that a change of scenery, with no discussion of religion, would help her, he planned for them to take a six-week trip to Niagara with Elizabeth's older sister Tryphena and her husband, Edward Bayard. During the visit, the group read and discussed Combe's *Constitution of Man and his Moral Philosophy* and many other intellectual works "all so rational and opposed to the old theologies." These books were critical of the religious ideas that had kept Elizabeth in so much fear. As her father hoped, Elizabeth became deeply interested in the new ideas, and her religious fears soon abated.

Chapter Two

Mrs. Elizabeth Cady Stanton

When she returned from Niagara, Elizabeth's interest in philosophy and other intellectual pursuits continued. Her brother-in-law Edward Bayard was a regular companion to Elizabeth and her sisters. Bayard studied law with Judge Cady. Elizabeth thought highly of him because he cared deeply about religious and spiritual matters. Bayard's approach to new ideas was to take nothing for granted and to continually ask questions. He treated the Cady sisters with respect and fostered their intellectual abilities.

Elizabeth was warm and humorous. She had a quick mind and friendly personality. Her sister Tryphena, Edward's wife, was much more quiet and introverted. Elizabeth enjoyed her discussions with Edward. Soon they grew closer and a romantic interest developed between them. Edward asked Elizabeth to run away with him. Although she was attracted to him, Elizabeth refused Edward's advances. It would devastate her sister, and Elizabeth had doubts that she wanted to be any man's wife. She knew from her father's law books that married women had no rights.

Once a year, Elizabeth took a trip to visit her older cousin Gerrit Smith and his wife, Nancy, in Peterboro, New York. The Smith's had a daughter, also named Elizabeth, or Libby, who was close to Elizabeth's age. The two Elizabeths became life-long, best friends. Unlike Elizabeth's father, "Cousin Gerrit" was a reformist who advocated the abolition of slavery. Elizabeth's family considered him a radical and did not approve of his ideas.

Cousin Gerrit was wealthy enough to invite guests to stay for several days, even weeks, at a time. Their spacious home was usually full of visitors from all over the country. Guests could expect to meet scholars, philosophers, philanthropists, judges, bishops, clergymen, and statesmen of both radical and conservative opinions at the Smith home. Lively conversations and thought-probing debates were favorite pastimes. For Elizabeth, the visit to her cousin's home was the highlight of her year.

Two reform issues were hotly debated at the Smith home: temperance and anti-slavery. In the nineteenth century "strong drink" was consumed at all times of the day. Brandy and cider were served at breakfast; beer, wine, and whiskey at dinner. "Rum breaks" were granted to workers the same way "coffee breaks" are today. Few social events were held without alcohol consumption. This resulted in a high level of alcoholism and the subsequent destruction often caused by excessive drink-

Elizabeth's cousin Gerrit Smith hosted gatherings of leading reformers at his home in Peterboro, N.Y. He is pictured here with other well-known reformers of the day (clockwise from Smith): Henry Ward Beecher, Charles Sumner, Wendell Phillips, Horace Greeley, Henry Wilson, and William Lloyd Garrison.

ing. The effort to outlaw the use of strong drink was called temperance.

Because it was only considered appropriate for men to drink, women became the strongest supporters of the temperance movement. Women had no protection if a husband drank up his wages and left the family without food, clothing, and shelter. Intoxicated husbands could beat their wives and children under protection of the law. The temperance movement continued to grow in strength throughout the nineteenth century.

The strongest reform movement of this era was anti-slavery. People who supported the effort to end slavery were called "abolitionists." Gerrit Smith hated slavery so much that he was willing to violate the law to help slaves escape to Canada. His mansion became one of the stations on the Underground Railroad, a network set up by abolitionists to help assist runaway slaves on their flight north to freedom. It provided runaway slaves with food, shelter, and assistance avoiding the authorities.

Once during a visit, Gerrit asked Elizabeth and Libby if they could keep a secret. When they agreed, he led them to a room on the third floor of his home where he introduced them to a light-skinned, black woman. Her name was Harriet. Harriet had just escaped from her master and was fleeing to Canada. Cousin Gerrit asked Harriet if she would tell the young women her story.

For two hours, Harriet told them the story of her childhood and youth. She had been taken from her family and sold for her beauty in a slave market in New Orleans at the age of fourteen. As she talked, Elizabeth and Libby wept. At the end of the day, Elizabeth and Libby were committed abolitionists.

Elizabeth later recalled Harriet's escape from New York:

> Dressed as a Quakeress, Harriet started at twilight with one of Mr. Smith's faithful clerks in a carriage for Oswego, there to cross the lake to Canada. The next day her master and the marshals from Syracuse were on her track in Peterboro, and traced her to Mr. Smith's premises. He was quite gracious in receiving them, and while assuring them that there was no slave there, he said that they were at liberty to make a thorough search of the house and grounds. He invited them to stay and dine and kept them talking as long as possible, as every hour helped Harriet to get beyond their reach...

Everyone at the Smith household was relieved when word later arrived that Harriet was safe with friends in Canada.

Elizabeth enjoyed the long hours of conversation and debate that began during the carriage rides to anti-slavery meetings held in the towns neighboring Peterboro. At those meetings, leading abolitionists, including William

Lloyd Garrison, Wendell Phillips, and Lucretia Mott spoke about emancipating slaves and the importance of individual rights. Elizabeth learned about the basic principles of American government and joined in the arguments over the best strategy to abolish slavery.

It was while visiting the Smiths for a month in 1839 that Elizabeth met Henry Brewster Stanton. Henry was an eloquent speaker at anti-slavery meetings and a guest at the Smith home. He was thirty-four, ten years older than Elizabeth, and tall with a large mustache. Henry had arrived at the Smith home accompanied by a young woman who was rumored to be his fiancé. Because she did not think he was "in the matrimonial market," Elizabeth relaxed during their conversations. They grew close. She admired his dedication to the anti-slavery movement. Soon she was attending as many of his speeches as she could.

Elizabeth learned that Henry Stanton was not engaged. One morning in October of 1839, he joined Elizabeth on the patio of the Smith home and invited her for a horseback ride. While walking their horses, Henry proposed marriage, and Elizabeth accepted.

Judge Cady strongly objected to Henry Stanton because he was an outspoken abolitionist who had no career prospects. Many of Elizabeth's friends opposed the engagement for the same reasons. And even Cousin Gerrit, feeling responsibility to Judge Cady because he had introduced Henry and Elizabeth, tried to change her mind.

Twenty-year-old Elizabeth Cady participated in meetings and debates over the abolition of slavery. (*From the archives of the Seneca Falls Historical Society.*)

Elizabeth had her own doubts, too. She was concerned about how he would treat her once they married. She knew how poorly the law protected wives. Feeling so much pressure about her decision to marry Henry, Elizabeth called off her engagement in February 1840. But Henry did not give up. He kept writing letters, explaining his beliefs and his plans for the future. He also wrote that in May he would be sailing to England to attend the first World's Anti-Slavery Convention in London. He would be abroad for eight months.

The idea of eight months and an ocean between them made Elizabeth realize that she loved Henry. She trusted him and did not want to be so far apart from him, regardless of what her family said. The couple eloped. In a simple, white dress, Elizabeth Cady married Henry Stanton on May 10, 1840. She insisted that the word "obey" be stricken from the marriage vows. She could not promise to "obey" a person she considered her equal. She also refused the custom of taking her husband's name. Most women at that time took their husband's full name, but Elizabeth refused to be called Mrs. Henry Stanton. She wanted to keep her maiden name and be called Mrs. Elizabeth Cady Stanton. There are no records that tell if any of her family attended the small ceremony.

Before sailing to London, Elizabeth and Henry visited Angelina and Sarah Grimké, sisters who were famous for speaking out against slavery. Because they made public speeches, the sisters were considered scandalous by some.

The sisters, who were friends of Henry Stanton, were charmed by Elizabeth.

In London, many of the delegates representing American anti-slavery societies were women. One was Lucretia Mott, a member of the Society of Friends, or the Quakers. She was twenty-two years older than Elizabeth and had long been a member of the Pennsylvania Anti-Slavery Society.

Lucretia's life experiences were quite different from Elizabeth's. Raised a Quaker, she was brought up in a faith that taught that men and women were equal in God's eyes. Her church and family encouraged free thinking and open discussions about religion, politics, and social reform. She was even allowed to preach—unheard of in any other denomination of the time. She refused to interpret the Bible literally. Her motto was "Seek Truth for Authority, not Authority for Truth."

When the convention opened on June 12, 1840, at Freemason's Hall in London, the women delegates were told they could not participate. They could stay but would have to sit in a separate section behind a closed curtain. A day-long debate ensued over what role the women would play at the convention.

Some of the male delegates argued strongly for the rights of the women to participate. George Bradburn said, "If anyone can prove to me that the Bible teaches the subjection of one half the human race to the other, then the best thing I could do for humanity would be to bring together every Bible in the universe and make a great bonfire of them." William Lloyd Garrison, who led the faction that wanted to include women, sat with the women.

Because Mr. Garrison was one of the first abolitionist leaders and something of a symbol of the worldwide anti-slavery movement, his actions spoke louder than words. Before he sat down with the women, he said, "After battling so many long years for the liberties of African slaves, I can take no part in a convention that strikes down the most sacred rights of all women. All of the slaves are not men."

Eventually, a vote was taken. Although he argued for their inclusion, Henry Stanton believed that the issue of women's rights would cloud the intention of the meetings. Henry's wavering predicted a tension in their marriage that would continue throughout their lives. From that moment on, Henry would refuse to unequivocally commit to the same issue that Elizabeth Cady Stanton would dedicate her life to resolving: women's rights.

This schism divided the anti-slavery movement as well. Henry's counterparts at the convention won the vote guaranteeing the women's right to participate. William Lloyd Garrison became the leader of the group who wanted to include women. Garrison's group also held the radical stance to completely abolish slavery. His opponents sought to only limit slavery by banishing it in the South and allowing the new western territories to decide for themselves.

That evening, Elizabeth and Lucretia Mott left the convention together. During their stay in London, the two women became good friends. Elizabeth admired the older woman's wisdom and experience and her dedication to social causes. They spent their spare time together walking through London and talking. They discussed the hypocrisy they encountered at the convention. How could the abolitionists fight so hard for the rights of slaves and give no thought to limiting the rights of women? Elizabeth and Lucretia decided that the struggle for freedom had to be much broader.

They decided to hold a convention and form a society when they returned home to talk about women's rights. They would discuss the following questions at their convention:

—Why were girls discouraged from obtaining a higher education?

—Why were women kept from holding meaningful, well-paying jobs?

—Why were married women and daughters who earned money from sewing or teaching paid less than men were and not even allowed to keep the money they earned?

—Why were a married woman and her children considered the legal property of her husband?

After several weeks in each other's company, Elizabeth

and Lucretia parted ways. They planned to meet again in the United States and begin organizing a women's rights convention. But it would be eight years before they were able to bring their plans to action.

Chapter Three

Seneca Falls, New York

After the London anti-slavery convention, Elizabeth and Henry boarded a steamer for a five-month tour of Europe. Henry wrote during their journey. He prepared essays about American abolitionism for two New York newspapers, the *New York American* and the *National Era*. Their tour of France was followed by several months in England, Ireland, and Scotland. Elizabeth enjoyed the trip. She had long wanted to see the birthplaces of the artists she admired and writers she had read. She and Henry visited battlefields and museums and toured libraries, art galleries, concert halls, and theaters.

In December 1840, they boarded an ocean steamer and spent "eighteen days, eleven hours, and fifteen minutes" on a "cold, rough, dreary voyage" home. Elizabeth had hoped her family's misgivings about her marriage would have subsided since their departure in May. Landing in Boston, they took the train to New York City in time to spend Christmas with her sister Harriet and her family. Then they headed to Johnstown to visit her parents.

Elizabeth was nervous about her father's welcome. He had been the one most against her marriage. But Judge Cady asked Henry to study law with him. To Elizabeth's great joy, Henry accepted. He would work for the judge for the next year and a half preparing to become a lawyer, and they would live at her parents' home.

Back home with her parents and sisters Margaret and Catherine, Elizabeth Cady Stanton spent the next year and a half taking walks, riding horses, and reading law, history, and political economy while Henry studied. She attended anti-slavery and temperance meetings and learned more about the way history and religion viewed women. She read the feminist writings of Mary Wollstonecraft and Lydia Maria Child. She also kept in regular contact with Lucretia Mott. She had not forgotten their vow to hold a women's rights convention.

Lucretia Mott had returned to Philadelphia and her husband and children, where she redoubled her efforts on behalf of abolition while managing a household of eight. Her home was regularly filled with guests, usually speakers attending anti-slavery meetings and fellow Quakers.

Motherhood and the duties of managing a growing household soon took up much of Elizabeth's time as well. On March 2, 1842, her son Daniel Cady Stanton was born. As Elizabeth later wrote, "The puzzling questions of theology and poverty that had occupied so much of my thoughts, now gave place to the practical one, 'what to do with a baby?' "

Elizabeth Cady Stanton would eventually become the mother of seven children. Her daughter Harriot, pictured here with Stanton in 1856, would follow in her mother's footsteps as an advocate of women's rights.

Elizabeth began reading the best books written about childcare. There she encountered some strange advice. Luckily for her baby, she relied on her common sense more than the "authorities." One book advised that babies should be bandaged tightly for fear that their soft bodies would fall apart. Elizabeth compared a baby's body to that of other animals, concluding that "it is very remarkable that kittens and puppies should be so well put together that they need not artificial bracing, and the human family be left wholly to the mercy of a bandage." Daniel remained unbandaged.

Elizabeth also refused to give her baby herbs for colic or insomnia. She opened the curtains to let the sunshine into the nursery and allowed him to regulate his own sleep. She did not make him wear a cap indoors and made sure his room was kept at sixty-five degrees, although conventional wisdom preached that unless a room was very warm, babies would catch cold and die. Elizabeth also strongly opposed the practice of spanking children when they cried. She believed that if a baby cried, there had to be a reason. She would not give her baby opium, although it was commonly used to insure infants slept through the night.

Elizabeth's father had bought a second home in the state capital of Albany in 1842. Elizabeth visited Albany often while Henry worked at the law office. She took an interest in the Married Women's Property Act, a piece of legislation supported by Governor William H. Seward.

First introduced in 1836, the bill would not be enacted until 1848.

The Married Women's Property Act proposed to allow a married woman to hold any property inherited or received as a gift in her own name. While in Albany, Elizabeth joined the governor and his wife in advocating the bill to members of the state senate and assembly. She believed it was important for women to have the right to protect their welfare by owning inheritances. The law was supported by some fathers and husbands who worried that family land and homes were threatened by debt collectors and greedy sons-in-law after the owner's death. If a wife could own some of the property, then that portion at least would be safe if business went bad or a son-in-law turned against his wife's family.

By the autumn of 1843, Henry was practicing law and becoming more involved in politics. The Stantons moved to Boston, where they boarded for some time with a Baptist minister. Elizabeth loved Boston. She socialized with activists and reformers, such as Lydia Maria Child, Nathaniel Hawthorne, Louisa May Alcott, James Russell Lowell, Wendell Phillips, and Frederick Douglass. She was also a frequent visitor at the home of William Lloyd Garrison. She attended lectures; anti-slavery meetings; churches; concerts; and temperance, peace, and prison-reform conventions. These meetings far surpassed any she had previously attended. The speeches, she wrote, were "eloquent and the debates earnest and forcible." She found the lectures of Mr. Theodore Parker, one of the great preachers of the time, so "soul-satisfying" that she attended as many as she could.

In March 1844, Elizabeth and Henry's second son, Henry Brewster Stanton, Jr., was born. Soon afterwards they moved into their first home (bought by Judge Cady) in Chelsea, a suburb of Boston. It had a view of the harbor and the surrounding country. Elizabeth began to take great pride in motherhood. She found it "a proud moment in a woman's life to reign supreme within four walls." She studied books about housekeeping and cooking, spending half of her time experimenting with new dishes. She felt the "same ambition to excel in all departments of the culinary art" that she had at school when learning different subjects. With the help of her two good servants, she put her entire house in order. Elizabeth welcomed her third son, Gerrit Smith Stanton, in September 1845.

Henry's health had declined and he could no longer take the harsh winters in Boston. In the spring of 1847, with many regrets, the family left Boston and moved to Seneca Falls, New York. Rural Seneca Falls, Elizabeth soon discovered, was much different than stimulating Boston. Here, the duties of motherhood and managing a household began to overwhelm her. Her house was older and less convenient. She had no close neighbors, and there were no concerts or lectures to attend. She grew depressed and frustrated.

Elizabeth discovered that many of the women in her

area were very poor. They raised children with husbands who drank too much, had little work, and no education. Realizing that these women had far less than she—not even the ability to escape by reading a book or a newspaper—greatly saddened her. She wrote:

> The general discontent I felt with woman's portion as wife, mother, housekeeper, physician, and spiritual guide . . . and the wearied, anxious look of the majority of women impressed me with a strong feeling that some active measures should be taken to remedy the wrongs of society in general, and of women in particular. My experience at the World's Anti-slavery Convention, all I had read of the legal status of women, and the oppression I saw everywhere, together swept across my soul, intensified now by many personal experiences. It seemed as if all the elements had conspired to impel me to some onward step. I could not see what to do or where to begin—my only thought was a public meeting for protest and discussion.

When Elizabeth received an invitation to have tea with her old friend Lucretia Mott at Jane Hunt's house, she eagerly accepted. She looked forward to discussing some of her new thoughts about the role of women in the family and in society.

Chapter Four

Women's Rights Convention

On July 13, 1848, Elizabeth had tea with four other women at Jane Hunt's home in nearby Waterloo, New York. She poured out her discontent with the plight of women, "with such vehemence and indignation that I stirred myself, as well as the rest of the party, to do and dare anything." That day, Elizabeth Cady Stanton, Lucretia Mott and her sister, Martha Coffin Wright, Jane Hunt, and Mary Ann McClintock decided to call a women's rights convention like the one that Elizabeth and Lucretia had promised each other eight years before in London. The very next day, Elizabeth posted a notice in the *Seneca County Courier*: "A convention to discuss the social, civil, and religious rights of woman will be held in the Wesleyan Chapel, Seneca Falls, New York, on Wednesday and Thursday, the 19th and 20th of July."

The following morning, the women met at Mary Ann McClintock's home to plan their convention. They decided that they needed to create a document that would set out the reasons for the convention. It was a difficult task. In 1848, there were 11 million women living in the

United States. How were they to express the grievances of all those women in one simple document? Then, while searching through the McClintock's' bookcase, Elizabeth came upon the Declaration of Independence. She read it aloud. Sitting at a mahogany table that is now housed in the Smithsonian Institute, the women changed "a phrase here and there" and wrote, "We hold these truths to be self-evident: that all men and women are created equal; that they are endowed by their Creator with certain inalienable rights; that among these are life, liberty and the pursuit of happiness . . ."

The five women added the following list of grievances:

a woman was denied the right to vote;

a woman was required to abide by laws without having a voice in forming the laws;

a woman lost all of her civil rights upon marriage;

a woman was required to accept her husband as her master;

a woman lost all rights to her children if her husband divorced or separated from her;

a woman lost all rights to her own property upon her marriage, even the right to keep or spend the wages she earned;

a woman was denied access to colleges;

a woman was forbidden to work in nearly all of the profitable jobs, and then was given only scanty wages for those jobs she was permitted to do;

a woman was required to abide by a different
code of morals than those required of a man;
a woman was put in a position subordinate
to a man within the church, as well as within
the state.

They titled their document "The Declaration of Sentiments."

For the next few days, Elizabeth worked on the list of
twelve resolutions that the group would present for passage at the convention. The resolutions called for actions
or changes in thinking. The effect of those actions or
changes in thinking would allow women to keep their
wages, go to college, own their own property, pursue
challenging careers, enjoy equality before the law, and
excercise free speech.

Wanting his legal opinion, Elizabeth asked Henry to
review her resolutions. Henry agreed with all of them,
until he reached the ninth resolution: "That it is the duty
of the women of this country to secure themselves their
sacred right to the elective franchise." Henry argued that
Elizabeth had gone too far. Elizabeth argued back, stating, "the power to make the laws is the right through
which we can secure all other rights." Henry was so
opposed to the ninth resolution that he threatened to leave
town during the convention rather than to be connected
to Elizabeth's scandalous resolution. Elizabeth would not
back down. Henry left Seneca Falls.

Elizabeth joined Lucretia Mott in the creation of the first women's rights convention, occuring in Seneca Falls, N.Y.

When the day of the convention arrived, Lucretia Mott was also shocked to read the ninth resolution. She feared they would be seen as going too far, too fast. Again, Elizabeth would not give in. Despite her concern, Lucretia agreed to support the resolution.

Three hundred people packed the small church. Charlotte Woodward was among one group of young women attending who were employed by the glove industry in Seneca Falls. The women did piecework to help support their families. But they had to work hidden away in their bedrooms because it was considered "unfitting" for a woman to be employed outside the home. "Most women," Charlotte later wrote,

> accepted this condition of society as normal and God-ordained and therefore changeless. But I do not believe that there was any community anywhere in which the souls of some women were not beating their wings in rebellion . . . Every fiber of my being rebelled, although silently, all the hours that I sat and sewed gloves for a miserable pittance which, after it was earned, could never be mine. I wanted to work, but I wanted to choose my task and I wanted to collect (and keep) my wages.

According to custom, Lucretia Mott's husband, James, stood as chairperson. All meetings and conventions at the time were chaired by men, even those that were exclusively female. James introduced the first speaker, Lucretia Mott. She was the only one of the five women who had any public speaking experience. Lucretia explained the reason for the convention and then called on Elizabeth. Elizabeth read the Declaration of Sentiments and the resolutions. Shock waves went through the crowd when she read the resolution calling for a woman's right to vote. There was much discussion and debate.

On the second day of the convention, the Declaration of Sentiments was unanimously adopted. Later that day, the resolutions were read and debated separately. Each resolution was adopted, except for the ninth. Elizabeth gave a powerful speech supporting this resolution. She was joined by Frederick Douglass, who argued that the right to vote was the basis for winning equal rights for women.

Following the speeches and debate, a vote on the ninth resolution was called. It barely passed. In the end, sixty-eight women and thirty-two men signed the Declaration of Sentiments. Of all the women signing the Declaration of Sentiments that day, only one—Charlotte Woodward—would be alive to cast her vote seventy-two years later when the 19th Amendment to the Constitution of the United States was finally ratified. The Women's Rights Convention at Seneca Falls marked the beginning of the women's rights movement.

Although Elizabeth considered the Women's Rights

Convention a huge success, the reactions to it were vehement. Headlines read, "Insurrection Among Women! The Petticoats Revolt!" The *Philadelphia Ledger* editorialized: "A woman is nobody. A wife is everything. A pretty girl is equal to ten thousand men, and a mother is, next to God, all powerful . . . [Elizabeth Cady Stanton is] a horrid monster . . . a professional lunatic."

Clergymen branded the convention blasphemous. The *Albany Advocate* went so far as to say that women's rights could bring about the end of the world. "The order of things established at the creation of mankind, and continued six thousand years, would be completely broken up . . ."

The criticism was so severe that many of the signers of the Declaration of Sentiments withdrew their support. Neighbors and friends gave Elizabeth and Lucretia the cold shoulder and claimed to have been disgraced by their involvement.

Yet in spite of the criticism, the movement spread. Two weeks later, a larger convention was held in Rochester. This time, a woman, Abigail Bush, chaired the meetings. Never again would a man run a woman's rights convention. Conventions were also held in Ohio, Indiana, Massachusetts, Pennsylvania, and New York City. Elizabeth wrote challenging letters to be read at the conventions she could not attend in person. To best prepare her letters to conventions, as well as to newspapers and friends, Elizabeth studied canon law, civil law, constitutions, Bibles,

Frederick Douglass supported the resolution for woman suffrage proposed by Elizabeth Cady Stanton at the 1848 women's rights convention in Seneca Falls, NY.

science, philosophy, and history. She soon found that with her mind again challenged and active, she no longer felt overwhelmed by the drudgery of household duties. But with Henry gone away on business much of the time, and no dependable servants, her roles as mother and homemaker still took up much of her time.

Also during 1848, the Married Women's Property Act that Elizabeth had worked for was finally passed. It was a very small step forward. For even after the bill passed, a wife had to ask her husband's permission to sell her property because women were not permitted to sign contracts. If the husband agreed to sell his wife's property he could still keep the money because he had signed the sales contract. If a wife wanted to leave her property to someone other than her husband, she had to have his approval because a married woman's will was invalid without her husband's signature. And a married woman still had no right to keep any money earned by her labor.

The bill was only a small step toward equal rights. But, although there was still a very long way to go, the publicity surrounding the passage of this bill mobilized some women who before had not fully realized the low regard in which the law held them.

Two years after the first Women's Rights Convention, in 1850, Elizabeth was thrilled to sign the announcement calling for the first National Women's Rights Convention. It was to be held in Worcester, Massachusetts. In addition to Elizabeth, William Lloyd Garrison, Mr. and

Mrs. Wendell Phillips, Gerrit Smith, Lucretia and James Mott, and Lucy Stone signed the announcement. Lucy Stone would soon become another major leader of the movement. Among those attending the convention were Angelina Grimké, whom Elizabeth had met shortly after her wedding; the first ordained female minister, Antoinette Brown; and advocate for abolition and women's rights, Sojourner Truth. Mrs. Paulina Wright Davis was the chairperson.

Mrs. Paulina Wright Davis had been left a wealthy widow after the death of her first husband. She decided to devote herself to improving the condition of women. Her primary focus had been counteracting most women's ignorance of their own bodies. She used a plaster figure of a female nude as her visual aid. This was considered so inappropriate that women frequently dropped their veils, ran out of the room, and even fainted. But, Paulina Wright Davis persisted. In a piece written for *The Una*, (one of the first women's rights publications) she wrote that to limit the number of children she bore and to have control over her body should be among a woman's most basic rights.

Elizabeth was unable to attend the 1850 National Women Right's Convention, but she sent a letter to be read on her behalf. The convention helped to sustain the momentum of the women's rights movement. It brought together over one thousand people from eleven states, many of whom had been working on their own for women's rights. The convention agreed to conduct a petition drive. They planned to deliver the signed petitions to the legislatures of eight states, hoping that the legislatures would give women the right to vote. They also agreed to hold a National Convention every year.

Chapter Five

Friendship for Life

Soon after the first National Women's Rights Convention, Elizabeth had her fourth son, Theodore Stanton. He was born February 10, 1851. Henry was away on business. Elizabeth wrote to Libby:

> Laugh in your turn. I have actually got my fourth son! Yes, Theodore Stanton bounded upon the stage of life with great ease—comparatively!! He weighed ten and one-half pounds. I was sick but a few hours, and did not lie down until half an hour before he was born, but worked round as hard as I could all night to do up the last things. At seven o'clock Sunday morning he was born. This morning I got up, bathed myself in cold water, and have sat by the table writing several letters.

Shortly after Theodore's birth, Elizabeth met Susan Brownell Anthony following an anti-slavery convention.

Born in Adams, Massachusetts, in 1820, Susan B. Anthony was five years younger than Elizabeth. Raised as a member of the Society of Friends, like Lucretia Mott, Susan's father, Daniel Anthony, believed in the equality of men and women. He made certain that both his sons and his daughters received a quality education. Susan even attended a boarding school for higher education in Philadelphia.

After working as a teacher for ten years, Susan became dissatisfied with the profession. She was paid too little. Women teachers, as a rule, received one-fourth the salary of men performing the same duties. Susan decided to leave teaching and devote herself to the temperance and anti-slavery movements. She was such an effective organizer and fund-raiser that she was soon made president of the Rochester Daughters of Temperance in New York.

Although Susan kept her eye on the women's rights movement in these early years, she was not convinced at first that it was where she should spend her time and energy. She thought the success of the temperance and anti-slavery movements would solve most of the issues raised in the women's movement. The temperance movement was very popular with women. Plus, because it was based on obvious religious principles, it was the only one considered proper for women to join.

It was not until Susan began to feel slighted because of her sex that she became dissatisfied with the politics of temperance. At one meeting, she was not allowed to

Susan B. Anthony left teaching to become one of the most instrumental reformers in the women's rights movement.

speak because the men believed it would be improper. She then turned her attention to the anti-slavery movement, thinking that with its focus on freedom it would be more inclusive.

In 1851, she was invited by her friend Amelia Bloomer to hear William Lloyd Garrison speak at an anti-slavery meeting in Seneca Falls. Amelia Bloomer was the assistant clerk at the Seneca Falls Post Office. Amelia was also a supporter of the temperance movement and publisher of *The Lily*, a newspaper "Devoted to the Interests of Women." But she was perhaps most well known for popularizing a new, and "scandalous," style of clothing for women. "Bloomers," as they came to be called, were ballooning trousers worn under knee-length skirts. Elizabeth Cady Stanton's cousin Libby had first introduced the style to Seneca Falls after seeing them worn in Switzerland. Amelia decided to publish patterns for making the clothing in her newspaper, and so the public named them for her. Wanting to hear Garrison, and secretly hoping to meet Elizabeth Cady Stanton and Lucretia Mott, Susan accepted Amelia's invitation.

At the conclusion of the anti-slavery meeting, Susan and Amelia were returning home when they ran into Elizabeth Cady Stanton and William Lloyd Garrison. Later, Elizabeth invited Susan to a meeting with Lucy Stone and Horace Greeley, the influential editor of the *New York Tribune*. This invitation sparked the beginning of a lifelong partnership between the two women.

Bloomers became a popular alternative to the cumbersome dresses of the nineteenth century among some reform-minded women.

Their fifty-year friendship created one of the most dynamic teams in the history of reform movements. Compiling her immense knowledge of law, literature, and philosophy with her readings of earlier feminists such as Mary Wollstonecraft, Elizabeth became the writer and philosopher of the women's rights movement. Susan was a highly skilled orator with phenomenal organizational and financial management skills. She was well travelled and accustomed to looking after details and became known as the "General" and strategist of the movement. Plus, as a mother of what would eventually be seven children, Elizabeth could not easily leave Seneca Falls. Susan, who remained unmarried, could spend weeks on end traveling, circulating petitions, and arranging meetings.

After one of her trips, Susan would stride across the Stanton lawn carrying a suitcase stuffed with scribbled notes and newspaper clippings. Elizabeth would use this information to create persuasive pamphlets and speeches. Susan, who disliked writing, tended to the children while Elizabeth worked.

Together they would review what Elizabeth had written. Then, with the documents ready and new events planned, Susan would set off again for several weeks of travel. As Elizabeth later said of their relationship:

> In thought and sympathy we were one, and in the division of labor we exactly complemented each

other. In writing we did better work than either could alone. While she is slow and analytical in composition, I am rapid and synthetic. I am the better writer, she the better critic. She supplied the facts and statistics, I the philosophy and rhetoric . . . Our speeches may be considered the united product of our two brains.

At times, however, their different roles became a point of contention. During the 1850s, when the children were small and Henry was away from home ten months out of the year, Elizabeth felt the full brunt of the domestic duties. At these times, Susan still expected Elizabeth to dedicate herself fully to their work. Elizabeth's time and energy were often sapped, and a strain could be felt between the two friends.

When Elizabeth's children were older, she made more speaking tours and concentrated on reform efforts. And in time, Elizabeth and Susan would focus solely on women's rights. But in the early years they worked as best they could, with Elizabeth writing speeches and Susan giving them. They worked in all three reform movements: temperance, abolition, and women's rights, because they believed that they were interrelated.

On April 20, 1852, Elizabeth was elected president of the Woman's State Temperance Convention. In her acceptance speech, Elizabeth attacked the laws that required a woman to remain the wife of a confirmed drunkard and that granted sole custody of her children to such a husband. She said, "Let no drunkard be the father of her children . . . Let us petition our State governments so to modify the laws affecting marriage, and the custody of children, that the drunkard shall have no claims on either wife or child." This was her first public criticism of marriage and child custody laws.

Churches and newspapers alike attacked Elizabeth for her comments. They accused her of wanting to do away with marriage and family. Elizabeth and her supporters knew this was not true but welcomed the controversy because it sparked discussion among men and women.

In June, while reactions to Elizabeth's speech were still strong, the Men's State Temperance Society held a convention in Syracuse. All temperance groups were invited to send delegates. The Women's State Temperance sent Susan B. Anthony and Amelia Bloomer. The women were treated terribly. One of the male participants described Susan and Amelia as a "hybrid species, half man and half woman, belonging to neither sex." He urged the group to condemn them, saying that the Women's Temperance Society and the women's rights movement "must be put down, cut up root and branch." The speech caused an uproar, and in the end, the women were excluded. For Elizabeth Cady Stanton and Susan B. Anthony, it was becoming difficult to support reform movements that did not support women's participation.

In September 1852, Susan attended the third National

Woman's Rights Convention in Syracuse. Elizabeth was at home awaiting the birth of her fifth child. Lucretia Mott presided and was elected the permanent president. Although her age and health would limit her active involvement to some extent, fifty-nine-year-old Lucretia Mott was the moral guide of the movement.

Over 2,000 people attended the third national convention. Susan read a letter Elizabeth had written for the occasion. Again, her ideas created controversy. She asked, "Should not all women living in States where a woman has the right to hold property refuse to pay taxes, so long as she is unrepresented in the government of that State?" One of the reasons for the Revolutionary War was taxation without representation. Were women not suffering the same injustice everyday? Secondly, Elizabeth demanded that women be admitted to the same jobs and professions as men. This meant, of course, that women deserved the same educational opportunities.

Her last argument was the most controversial. She posited that instead of making a woman "noble and free," religion ". . . has made her bondage but more certain and lasting, her degradation more helpless and complete." Elizabeth was convinced that the church, after teaching for centuries that a woman should serve husband and father, was one of the greatest barriers to equal rights for women. This criticism of religion was controversial both inside and outside of the movement.

One month after the convention, Elizabeth and Henry

had their first daughter, Margaret Livingston Stanton. Elizabeth was just one month shy of her thirty-seventh birthday. Her daughter weighed twelve pounds at birth, and Elizabeth was up and about in no time.

With five children to care for, Elizabeth felt blessed when she found Amelia Willard. Amelia was a Quaker woman, with ideals similar to Elizabeth's, who became the Stanton's faithful housekeeper for the next thirty years. Elizabeth considered Amelia ". . . a treasure, a friend and comforter, a second mother to my children, who understood all life's duties and gladly bore its burdens . . . But for this noble, self-sacrificing woman, much of my public work would have been quite impossible. If by word or deed I have made the journey of life easier for any struggling soul, I must in justice share the meed of praise accorded me with my little Quaker friend, Amelia Willard."

Amelia felt that her greatest possible contribution to the women's rights movement was to help care for the Stanton children and household so that Elizabeth had more time to devote to her writings and speeches.

Chapter Six

Fighting for Women's Rights

In the early weeks of 1854, Elizabeth, with Susan's help, prepared a speech to be delivered to the New York State Legislature. It would be the first time a woman spoke before the state legislative body. The speech urged the legislature to revise the Married Women's Property Act. The revisions to the Married Women's Property Act would guarantee a woman the right to keep her own earnings, to share guardianship of her children with her husband, and to keep her property if she were widowed. Elizabeth would also present a petition for women's suffrage.

Elizabeth asked Judge Cady to read her speech. Although she wanted his approval, she also knew that he was unsympathetic toward the women's rights movement and disapproved of her leadership in it. She nervously sat opposite him in his study and read her speech.

Elizabeth noticed tears in her father's eyes, and realizing that she had touched his heart, she began reading more confidently. When she finished, Judge Cady said nothing. Elizabeth could hear her own heart beating in the silence of the room. Then, her father said, "Surely you have had a happy, comfortable life, with all your wants and needs supplied; and yet that speech fills me with self-reproach; for one might naturally ask, how can a young woman, tenderly brought up, who has had no bitter personal experience, feel so keenly the wrongs of her sex? Where did you learn this lesson?"

Elizabeth responded, "I learned it here, in your office, when I was a child, listening to the complaints women made to you. They who have sympathy and imagination to make the sorrows of others their own can readily learn all the hard lessons of life from the experiences of others."

Judge Cady was quiet and then complimented Elizabeth for having made her points "clear and strong." He said that he could find her "even more cruel laws than those you have quoted." He also suggested some improvements to her speech, working with her until one o'clock in the morning. But Elizabeth never knew how he really felt about women's rights. He never said anything in favor of it or against it. She did not know if her speech altered his opinion.

On February 14, 1854, Elizabeth stood before the crowded New York State Legislature. Most of the politicians had never seen a woman give a speech. Elizabeth was dressed in a black silk dress trimmed in white lace. She looked very ladylike.

In her address, Elizabeth described the inferior position of women under New York law. She talked about many of the issues first raised in the Declaration of Sentiments. To answer the question, "What do women want?" she said:

> Let us say, in behalf of the women of this State, we ask for all that you have asked for yourselves, in the progress of your development, since the Mayflower cast anchor beside Plymouth Rock; and simply on the ground that the rights of every human being are the same and identical.

Elizabeth gave a powerful speech, but the legislature did not pass the amendments. One assemblyman rejected her argument by stating that God had created men and women unequally: "A higher power than that from which emanates legislative enactments has given forth the mandate that man and woman shall not be equal." Although others sympathized with her, Senator Seward, the former governor of New York who supported the passage of the original bill, explained, ". . . You had the argument, but custom and prejudice are against you, and they are stronger than truth and logic."

Men were not the only opposition Elizabeth faced that day. Many of the women who attended were also antagonistic. Trying to prove that women's rights were anti-family, one of them asked Elizabeth what she did with her children while she gave speeches. Elizabeth replied:

Ladies, it takes me no longer to speak to you than you to listen. What have you done with your children the two hours you have been sitting here? But, to answer your question, I never leave my children to go to Saratoga, Washington, Newport, or Europe, or even to come here. They are, at this moment, with a faithful nurse at Delevan House. Having accomplished my mission, we shall all return home together.

Elizabeth faced criticism from women throughout her lifetime. Although it was common practice for wealthy women to leave their children with nurses while they vacationed, the fact that these same women assumed that Elizabeth's children were neglected while she worked for equality infuriated her. She realized she not only had the difficult task of changing men's minds about women, but also exposing the prejudice of her own sex. Susan made tens of thousands of copies of Elizabeth's speech for distribution.

After her 1854 speech to the New York Legislature, Elizabeth was invited to deliver paid lectures on the Lyceum Bureau Lecture circuit. In this era before television, telephones, or radios, lectures were both a form of entertainment and a means of learning about current issues. Hearing of her invitation to join the lecture circuit, Elizabeth's father declared that he would disinherit her if she persisted. "Your first lecture will be a very expensive one," he threatened. She responded, "I intend that it shall be a very profitable one." Elizabeth was hurt by her father's reaction, not because of the inheritance, but as she wrote to Susan:

> I passed through a terrible scourging when last at my father's. I cannot tell you how deep the iron entered my soul. I never felt more keenly the degradation of my sex. To think that all in me of which my father would have felt a proper pride had I been a man, is deeply mortifying to him because I am a woman. That thought has stung me to a fierce decision—to speak as soon as I can do myself credit. But the pressure on me just now is too great.

On January 20, 1856, Elizabeth and Henry's sixth child was born. She was named Harriot Eaton Stanton, and she would eventually become a suffragist herself. Although Elizabeth now had an infant, the majority of her children were older and more independent. Daniel and Henry had been sent to boarding school, and with help from Amelia Willard, Elizabeth was free to write her speeches with new fervor.

Elizabeth's speeches advocated women's rights in marriage and the legal system. She supported divorce as an acceptable alternative to an unhappy marriage. She argued that without the right to vote, women would never be equal citizens. She was also concerned with improving a woman's quality of life through better education and the sharing of domestic duties with husbands.

On March 14, 1859, Elizabeth gave birth to her last child, Robert. This time, her recovery took longer than usual. Soon afterwards, she received news that her father was sick. Elizabeth sat with him during his last few months, spending countless hours reading to him and relieving her mother of other nursing chores. Judge Daniel Cady died October 31, 1859. He was eighty-six years old. At some point, he had restored Elizabeth's inheritance of $50,000. After he died, Elizabeth was content to know that he loved her and that he was proud of her courage and determination, although they never did see eye-to-eye on women's rights.

During the late 1850s, the movement had begun to receive larger contributions from supporters. These donations increased the movement's credibility. In 1858, Francis Jackson, a wealthy Boston abolitionist, donated $5,000 because of the suffering his married daughter had endured under the existing laws. In 1859, Charles F. Hovey, another wealthy Boston reformer and philanthropist, left financial support to several reform movements. His will stated that the income from a $50,000 fund was to be distributed annually to reform movements, with much of it going to anti-slavery and women's rights. When slavery was abolished, that portion was reallocated to women's rights. Equally significant were the twenty-five dollar contributions from many individuals.

In March 1860, Elizabeth again addressed the New York State Legislature in support of yet another amendment to the Married Women's Property Act. Elizabeth's speech, "A Slave's Appeal," explained that married women, like slaves, did not use their own names, had no right to their children, could not keep their earnings, could not purchase property, and could not sign contracts. "The prejudice against color...is no stronger than that against sex," said Elizabeth. Her speech was so moving that her points were heard on their merits. The Married Women's Property Act of 1860 passed the next day. This new law provided sweeping changes for women's rights, becoming a model for similar laws that were adopted in other states.

Social changes were slowly beginning to take place. Soon after the law had passed, a woman brought a complaint against her husband, a drunkard who wanted to take away their two children. The husband's lawyer, who had not yet heard of the new law, cried out, "Well, we claim our paramount rights—that the father shall have custody of the children." The judge informed the lawyer that those "paramount rights" he claimed for his client were a thing of the past. In view of the new law the judge said, "I cannot take the children away from the mother; she has just as much right to them as her husband."

With these significant rights secured for married women, Elizabeth turned her energies to the issue of divorce. She chose the opening session of the tenth annual National Woman's Rights Convention, held in May 1860 in New York City, to introduce her ideas.

Just as the delegates had settled into their seats, Elizabeth jolted them by introducing ten resolutions recommending that divorce laws be liberalized. She stated that divorce laws should be made easier so that unhappy marriages could be dissolved. She argued that a woman should not be forced to stay in a dangerous and loveless marriage because her husband demanded it.

Her words fell like a cannon ball onto the convention floor. Immediately, Antoinette Blackwell stood and offered thirteen resolutions in opposition to Elizabeth's ten. Wendell Phillips was so opposed to Elizabeth's resolutions that he made a motion to strike them out of the convention minutes altogether. Susan B. Anthony and Lucretia Mott defended her. Lucy Stone spoke in favor of Antoinette Blackwell. The debate continued long after the convention. Many newspapers accused Elizabeth of wanting to do away with marriage in favor of "free love."

Worse yet, newspapers portrayed all of the women's rights leaders as spinsters, too unattractive to get husbands. They argued that women's rights organizers were trying to stir up discontent among "normal, happily married" women. Susan B. Anthony published a report showing that of the original leaders of the women's rights movement, only she had never been married. The other sixteen married leaders had a combined total of thirty-six children. They were hardly the "dried-up old maids," or

Newspaper editor Horace Greeley attacked Elizabeth Cady Stanton for her views on divorce.

"mummified and fossilated females, void of domestic duties, habits and natural affections," that the press portrayed.

Even still, Elizabeth Cady Stanton's views on divorce were radical, and they began to split the movement into two factions. Stanton and her followers supported a more expansive claim to women's rights. The other group, led by Lucy Stone, wanted to limit their efforts to suffrage. Although she occasionally thought that Elizabeth's positions were radical and her pronouncements rash, Susan B. Anthony publicly defended her. Privately they debated the prudence of broadening the movement's platform to include divorce legislation.

Elizabeth's stand on divorce was costing the women's rights movement the support of many male advocates as well. Horace Greeley, the powerful editor of the *New York Tribune* and famous abolitionist, turned his newspaper against Elizabeth and her views on divorce. Supporters, such as Garrison and Wendell Phillips, did not protest Greeley's attacks. It was becoming clear that Elizabeth and Susan needed to forge new alliances to achieve their goals for women's rights.

As these tensions developed within the women's rights movement, the debate over slavery was reaching a climax. In 1859, the abolitionist John Brown had led a bloody raid in Virginia against the United States Arsenal at Harpers Ferry. The effects of this violence spread north and south. Soon the issue of women's rights was buried beneath the immediacy of civil war.

Chapter Seven

Civil War and Reconstruction

On November 6, 1860, Abraham Lincoln was elected president of the United States. Shortly thereafter, South Carolina seceded from the Union. Soon the other states of the deep and upper south voted to break their bonds with the United States.

The Civil War put the women's rights movement on hold as wives, mothers, and daughters became involved in the war effort. They organized relief and medical aid. They collected food and clothing and distributed it to the needy. They worked as nurses in hospitals, cared for the sick and wounded in their own homes, made bandages, and fought to improve the sanitary conditions in the army camps. Women took on the jobs vacated by the men who went off to fight, and for the first time, they were hired in government offices. These activities gave women organizational experience and a new public voice. Women began caring for themselves and managing businesses and family affairs without relying on men. As the men saw firsthand the capabilities of women, it seemed as if the war would provide the women's rights movement with the respect it needed to complete its goals.

In the spring of 1862, Elizabeth Cady Stanton moved to New York City to join her husband, who had served as deputy collector for the Port Authority since August of the previous year. In New York, the war seemed more real to her than in rural Seneca Falls. She threw herself into the effort. She hoped that emancipation of slaves would lead to emancipation of women.

Susan B. Anthony thought it was a mistake to give up women's rights activism during the war. Anthony, who lived with the Stantons in New York, did not think that freeing the slaves would have a positive impact on women's rights. But she found no support from Elizabeth and the other leaders, such as Lucretia Mott, to continue their work for women during the war. Susan finally conceded. Later it became clear that her fears were correct.

On January 1, 1863, President Lincoln issued the Emancipation Proclamation. It promised freedom to the slaves in the Confederate states. It did not free the slaves in the Union states of Maryland, Missouri, West Virginia, Tennessee, Kentucky, and Delaware. This distinction motivated Elizabeth and Susan to call a meeting in May 1863 to form a new organization called the Woman's National Loyal League. The goal of this new league was to gather a million signatures to a petition asking for an anti-slavery amendment—the Thirteenth Amendment—

Although they had differing attitudes towards the Civil War, Elizabeth and Susan worked tirelessly together to help end slavery.

to the Constitution of the United States. Elizabeth was elected president of the Woman's National Loyal League, and Susan was named secretary.

Susan and Elizabeth worked tirelessly for fifteen months to gather signatures on petitions supporting the Thirteenth Amendment. By August 1864, the league had gathered over 400,000 signatures and 5,000 members. The petitions for the Thirteenth Amendment were presented to Congress by Charles Sumner, the outspoken anti-slavery senator from Massachusetts, on February 1, 1865, and ratified that same year on December 18.

Soon, abolitionists realized that the Thirteenth Amendment freed slaves but did nothing to guarantee their rights. Work began on the Fourteenth Amendment to protect the rights of all "male" citizens, regardless of race. This issue became part of the Republican platform in 1866. Elizabeth and Susan became furious when they saw the word "male" included in the draft. Never before had "male" been used instead of "citizen" or "people" in the Constitution. They looked to their abolitionist friends for support and agreed to work with Theodore Tilton, the editor of the *New York Independent*, and Wendell Phillips to merge the anti-slavery societies with the women's rights movement into one organization with universal suffrage as its platform.

At the eleventh National Women's Rights Convention held May 10, 1866, Susan introduced a resolution to unite the two movements into the American Equal Rights

Association (AERA). Lucretia Mott was elected president, and Elizabeth was elected vice president, who said: ". . . Has not the time come, Mr. President, to bury the black man and the woman in the citizen, and our two organizations in the broader work of reconstruction?" The convention adjourned to meet in Boston on May 31.

In Boston, Wendell Phillips stated that suffrage was the great question of the hour. He then brought up a nagging dilemma that had been growing within the new association: Was it more important for African-American men to vote than women? Phillips said, ". . . in view of the peculiar circumstances of the Negro's position, his claim to this right might fairly be considered to have precedence." He continued, however, ". . . To prevent such a corruption of the National Constitution as well as for the general welfare of the community, male and female, I wish to excite interest everywhere in the maintenance of women's right to vote." But, one month after the AERA was founded, Congress passed the Fourteenth Amendment without change and sent it on to the states for ratification.

Elizabeth and Susan wrote petitions and collected 10,000 signatures to remove the word "male" from the Fourteenth Amendment. In October, Elizabeth even offered herself as a candidate for Congress in order "to test the constitutional right of a woman to run for office." In a public letter proclaiming her candidacy, Elizabeth wrote, ". . . Belonging to a disenfranchised class, I have no political antecedents to recommend me to your support, but my creed is *free speech, free press, free men,* and *free trade,*—the cardinal points of democracy." Elizabeth received only twenty-four votes.

Support for woman suffrage was waning. Leading abolitionists, including Tilton and Phillips, withdrew their support declaring it was "the Negro's hour." Frederick Douglass said, "I must say that I do not see how anyone can pretend that there is the same urgency in giving the ballot to woman as to the Negro." Even Elizabeth's cousin Gerrit Smith agreed that women should wait.

In 1867, the state of New York agreed to hold a convention to consider striking the word "male" from the state constitution. Elizabeth and Susan initiated another massive campaign and traveled the state, as Susan put it, "like the flying shuttle in the loom of the weaver." One of Susan's stops was to visit Mrs. Horace Greeley, the wife of the *Tribune* editor. Mrs. Greeley signed one of the petitions. A supporter of the Republican party, Greeley was deeply embarrassed by his wife's petition and blamed Susan and Elizabeth. He abruptly terminated any further support to the women's rights movement. On July 25, 1867, the amendment to strike the word "male" from the state constitution went down in defeat.

Disheartened, Susan and Elizabeth accepted Senator Samuel Wood's invitation to rally support for woman suffrage in Kansas that summer. They traveled 1500 miles to urge support of two referendums: one, to remove the word "male" from the voting requirements in the state constitution, and two, to remove the word "white." Lucy Stone and her husband had spent April and May distributing leaflets in Kansas urging both propositions.

As Elizabeth later described one leg of their journey to Kansas:

> We had a low, easy carriage, drawn by two mules, in which we stored about a bushel of tracts, two valises, a pail for watering the mules, a basket of apples, crackers, and other such refreshments as we could purchase on the way. Some things were suspended underneath the carriage, some packed on behind, and some under the seat and at our feet...As we went to the very verge of civilization, wherever two dozen voters could be assembled, we had a taste of pioneer life. We spoke in log cabins, in depots, unfinished schoolhouses, churches, hotels, barns, and in the open air.

In order to cover more territory, the women split up to spread their message. Both referendums lost, however, and they became further disillusioned.

While in Kansas, Elizabeth and Susan accepted the help of George Francis Train. Train, a Democrat from St. Louis, was a rich, erratic, highly effective, and colorful speaker. Mr. Train believed in such "radical heresies" as an eight-hour work day, organized labor, paper money, and, of course, woman's suffrage. Mr. Train offered to pay for a speaking tour and to give Susan and Elizabeth money to start a woman's suffrage paper. They readily accepted his offers, and on January 1, 1868, the first issue of their paper, *The Revolution*, appeared. The paper's motto was: "Men, their rights, and nothing more; women, their rights, and nothing less." They did not accept advertisements for any products they did not believe in. Elizabeth described the brief period while she edited *The Revolution* as "the happiest of my life, and I may add, the most useful." A publication of its own was what the movement needed.

The Fourteenth Amendment was ratified in 1868. It was clear to Elizabeth that the Federal government did not intend to grant women the right to vote. This angered her and she adopted an anti-male attitude, alienating many lukewarm supporters, among them her cousin Gerrit Smith. During this year, she also bought a home in Tenafly, New Jersey, with the money her father had left her. Henry Stanton kept his home in New York with their son Daniel. The move for Elizabeth was a show of independence. She chose her house and bought it with her own money. At age fifty-three, she began to dedicate herself to the cause of women's rights with an enthusiasm that earlier domestic obligations had not allowed.

A decisive split occurred in the women's movement on May 11, 1869, at the convention of the American

George Francis Train allocated money for Elizabeth and Susan to publish *The Revolution*.

Equal Rights Association. The debate centered around the Fifteenth Amendment which had been passed by Congress in February. The amendment gave African-American males the right to vote. When the AERA voted to endorse the amendment, Susan and Elizabeth took it upon themselves to announce the formation of the National Woman's Suffrage Association. Elizabeth was to serve as president and Susan as one of the members of the Executive Committee. Joining with Elizabeth and Susan were, among others, Lucretia Mott, Martha C. Wright, and Elizabeth's cousin Libby Miller. Believing that the "male betrayal" had undermined their efforts in the past, they voted that no men would be allowed to join the new association. They would focus their efforts on securing passage of a woman suffrage amendment.

Lucy Stone, believing that it was the "hour of the Negro," stated her belief that women would have to wait. She and many other abolitionists formed a separate group called the American Woman Suffrage Association. This split in the women's movement would last for twenty years.

By 1870, Elizabeth Cady Stanton had grown frustrated with the disharmony within the reform movement. She decided to give up going to conventions for the time and to concentrate instead on giving public lectures. She became a paid lecturer for the Lyceum Bureau Lecture circuit, traveling from Maine to Texas and west to California, speaking steadily eight months out of the year for

Lucy Stone became the leader of a faction of reformers who rallied for ex-slaves' rights, hoping the same rights would be later granted to women.

the next decade. Meanwhile, Susan B. Anthony was busy with the suffrage association. She also worked to pay off the $10,000 debt incurred from running *The Revolution*. Anthony resented Stanton's absence from what she thought was the real work of reform and her friend's refusal to help pay any of the debt from a paper they had jointly run.

On September 15, 1871, Elizabeth's mother, Margaret Livingston Cady, died. Elizabeth had returned to Johnstown to care for her for the last two weeks of her life.

In 1870, a woman named Victoria Woodhull announced that she would run for president of the United States in the 1872 election. Once a professional medium, Woodhull was an independent and flamboyant newcomer to the fight for women's rights. She was also trailed by a long history of scandal. Her liberal views on divorce brought accusations of promiscuity. Even worse, she was a self-defined supporter of "free love." She had opened a stock brokerage firm on Wall Street with her sister Tennessee, ran her own newspaper, and in 1871 addressed Congress, where she argued that the first section of the Fourteenth Amendment gave women the right to vote. In it, the right to vote is granted to "all persons born or naturalized in the United States." It followed, she argued, that the document clearly granted women the right to vote.

Susan B. Anthony had been in the audience during Woodhull's speech, and afterward, she invited her to the upcoming annual woman's suffrage convention in Wash-

Elizabeth made a drastic error in judgement when she supported Victoria Woodhull's presidential ambitions.

ington. In May, Elizabeth Cady Stanton followed Anthony's lead and invited Woodhull to the National Woman Suffrage Association convention in New York City.

The press claimed that the allegiance with Woodhull only proved that the National Association was immoral and unnatural. Lucy Stone and the American Association denied any ties to Woodhull. Under this pressure, Anthony began to fear that Woodhull could destroy all their hard work. She advocated severing their ties with Woodhull once and for all. But Elizabeth Cady Stanton would not hear of it.

In May 1872, at the National Woman's Suffrage Association's convention, Victoria Woodhull tried to convene the organization as a meeting of the Equal Rights Party, the same party that would nominate her upcoming candidacy for president. Anthony opposed the motion, and managed to move a majority to her view. Stanton, however, supported Woodhull's presidential ambitions.

Angered by what she considered to be a desertion of her cause by women leaders, Woodhull exposed an affair between Elizabeth Tilton (the wife of Theodore Tilton), and the famous Reverend Henry Ward Beecher, who had spoken out against her from his pulpit. Woodhull also claimed that Elizabeth Cady Stanton had verified the story. Elizabeth publicly defended Mrs. Tilton and cut off contact with Victoria Woodhull. She realized that Susan B. Anthony had been right to warn of the danger a person like Woodhull posed to the movement.

Over the next decade there were more setbacks for the women's suffrage movement. Surprisingly, many resulted from the temperance movement and the increasing number of factory jobs filled by women—two social changes that were responsible for getting women involved in the women's rights movement in the first place.

Women who had never considered voting joined the temperance movement. More and more women picketed saloons and liquor stores. Churchgoers knelt in prayer on saloon floors. Between 1873 and 1874, 3,000 saloons closed. These successes led to the growth of the Women's Christian Temperance Union and money and volunteers flowed in. Its president, Frances Willard, was a friend of Susan B Anthony's. Frances succeeded in getting the organization to expand its goals to include women's suffrage under the Home Protection Program.

Wealthy alcohol interests worried that if women were given the right to vote, they would vote to stop alcohol sales. Brewers, saloonkeepers, and "strong drink" salesmen poured money into the campaigns of legislator's who opposed women's suffrage. Many big business leaders were also opposed to women's suffrage. They thought that women would be more inclined to vote for candidates who supported laws guaranteeing workers higher wages and safer factories.

In November 1872, Susan B. Anthony decided to test the argument that the Fourteenth Amendment had given women the right to vote. She voted in Rochester, New York. Two weeks later, she was arrested. She was not allowed to testify on her own behalf, and the judge found her guilty and charged her a $100 fine that she refused to pay.

In 1875, the Supreme Court gave the women's suffrage movement a blow when it ruled that the right to vote was governed by the state, and that the Constitution only protected against discrimination based on race, not gender. Although this was a setback at the time, the decision did give the suffrage movement a focus for the next thirty-five years. It was clear that the only way women would be allowed to vote in the United States was if an amendment guaranteeing that right was added to the federal Constitution.

Despite its failure on the federal level, women's suffrage was successful in some of the territories and states. The territory of Wyoming gave women the right to vote in 1869, as did Colorado in 1893. Utah and Idaho followed suit in 1896. It would be more than two decades, however, before women could legally vote in any of the eastern states.

The 1875 Supreme Court ruling also changed Elizabeth Cady Stanton's focus. At sixty years old, she felt that the younger women could better lead the fight for the voting amendment. She wanted to devote her time to other issues that interested her, mainly fairer divorce laws, religious reform, sexuality issues, and birth control.

Elizabeth doubted that woman suffrage would provide the far-reaching reform she advocated. What would voting do for women if they were not free to live their own lives and make their own decisions? She wanted women to think more critically about traditional gender roles in marriage and religion, and she wanted women and men to talk about these controversial subjects.

Elizabeth thought that women and men deserved to be in respectful, fulfilling marriages. She urged women to stand up for their happiness and to question the idea that a wife's sole purpose in life was to serve her husband. How interesting it would be, she proposed to husbands, to be married to a woman who was vitally interested in a variety of topics rather than just fashion, dinner guest lists, and household management.

She believed that if a marriage turned out badly, then it should be ended without requiring a "guilty" party and public discussion of personal problems. Elizabeth urged legislators to adopt more liberal divorce laws. If a divorce were granted, the mother should be given equal consideration for custody of the children.

Elizabeth believed women should educate themselves about their own bodies, especially the reproductive cycle. She freely spoke in favor of contraception. She wrote, "I did not see [when young] all that I now see with age and experience . . . I then knew no better than to have seven children in quick succession." She also believed that husbands and wives should talk more openly about sex.

Chapter Eight

Grand Old Woman

On November 11, 1880, Lucretia Mott died. Elizabeth felt this loss deeply. Mott had been her friend and colleague since their meeting in London forty years before. The next day, on her sixty-fifth birthday, Elizabeth began writing a diary. She and Susan B. Anthony started a book project to commemorate their life's work. It was entitled *History of Woman Suffrage*. Over the years, Susan had saved every document, convention record, and newspaper clipping about the movement, and together they sorted and arranged the material. The first volume was published in May 1881, and the second volume was completed in 1882.

When she shifted her focus from women's suffrage, Elizabeth began speaking and writing about her more controversial ideas, such as the ones on marriage, reproduction, and sexuality. But nothing that Elizabeth said or did was as controversial as her opinions on the damaging role that traditional Christianity played in women's lives. Elizabeth said that traditional Christianity taught women to be self-sacrificing and hampered independent development. Christianity, she argued, taught women that Eve had brought sin into the world and therefore all women were condemned by God "to remain in a state of remorseful atonement for Eve's original sin." She would later culminate her ideas about women and religion in *The Woman's Bible*.

Elizabeth Cady Stanton began writing *The Woman's Bible* in the late 1880s. Her outline began to take shape as she set sail to England on October 27, 1886, to spend time with her daughter Harriot and her family. She was sixteen days shy of her seventy-first birthday. Her objective was to show that many of the original texts of the Bible had not been translated or interpreted accurately. She would mark each chapter of the Bible that in any way referred to women. Then she would cut out the texts, pasting them at the top of a page, and underneath write her own interpretation. She said, "the Bible was no more and no less than the history and legends of a people as they searched for God." Seven other women eventually assisted Elizabeth in the decade-long project.

While still in England, Elizabeth received a cablegram from New York that her husband, Henry, had died at age eighty-one. All that day, January 12, 1887, Elizabeth and Harriot sat and talked about life and death. Elizabeth recalled how proud she was of her husband when he was a young abolitionist orator. She talked about their forty-six years of marriage and their long separations. Although they had long ago lost the "joy of deep soul-love," as Elizabeth put it, she had cared for him deeply.

That spring, Elizabeth went to Paris to spend time with her son Theodore and his family. Theodore had taken an interest in women's rights and just published his second book on the subject. His first book had been titled *The Woman Question in Europe.*

Elizabeth spent six months in Paris, attending concerts, operas, theater, and touring the area. In late October, she returned to England. There she received a summons from Susan B. Anthony to return to America to help with the planning for the 1888 International Council of Women. Unlike the Seneca Falls Convention forty-two years before, the International Council of Women Convention was a well-planned event. Held from March 25 to April 1 in Washington, D.C., it was attended by representatives from fifty-three organizations, trades, professions, and reform movements, and eighty speakers and delegates from the United States, Canada, England, Ireland, France, Norway, Finland, Denmark, and India. Even United States President Grover Cleveland and First Lady Frances Folsom Cleveland were among those who welcomed the delegates.

Two years later, in February 1890, the two United States suffrage associations finally reunited into one—the National American Woman Suffrage Association. Elizabeth was elected president. She had earned the reputation of being both the matriarch and the radical

Henry Brewster Stanton died on January 12, 1887.

reformer of the movement. She always wore a black silk dress with a white lace collar and looked very proper, maternal, and by now, quite heavy. Her election was not unanimous because of her outspoken positions on divorce, birth control, and religion. Anthony was elected vice-president-at-large.

On November 15, 1891, Elizabeth Cady Stanton celebrated her seventy-sixth birthday in New York City with her children. She had sold her house in Tenafly and now stayed with family and friends. Her health had begun to deteriorate, and she suffered from lameness and heart disease.

On January 17 through 21, 1892, the annual National American Woman Suffrage Convention was held in Washington, D.C. At the same time, the woman's suffrage bill was reintroduced to Congress. As president of the National American Woman Suffrage Association, Elizabeth prepared an address to the Congressional Judiciary Committee.

Instead of repeating her usual arguments, Elizabeth's speech presented her philosophical reasons for the need for equal rights. She argued that every individual—man or woman—is essentially isolated. Therefore, everyone must be prepared to live with his or her "self," first and foremost, before they can live with another. The words she used came from her own experiences. She spoke of the "individuality of each human soul," saying:

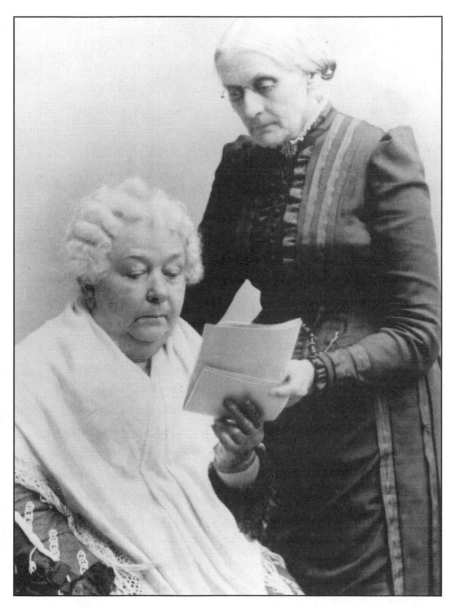

Elizabeth Cady Stanton and Susan B. Anthony worked together toward reform for half a century.

. . . In discussing the sphere of man, we do not decide his rights as an individual, as a citizen, as a man, by his duties as a father, a husband, a brother or a son . . . The isolation of every human soul and the necessity of self-dependence must give each individual the right to choose his own surroundings. The strongest reason for giving woman all the opportunities for higher education, for the full development of her faculties, her forces of mind and body; for giving her the most enlarged freedom of thought and action; a complete emancipation from all forms of bondage, of custom, dependence, superstition; from all the crippling influences of fear—is the solitude and personal responsibility of her own individual life. The strongest reason we ask for woman a voice in the government under which she lives; in the religion she is asked to believe; equality in social life, where she is the chief factor; a place in the trades and professions, where she may earn her bread, is because of her birthright to self-sovereignty; because, as an individual, she must rely on herself.

"The Solitude of Self" was published in the Congressional Record and immediately reproduced and distributed as a pamphlet. She gave the speech again at the opening session of the National American Woman Suffrage Association Convention. Soon after, Elizabeth Cady

Elizabeth Cady Stanton became the "Grand Old Woman" of the women's rights movement.
(*From the archives of the Seneca Falls Historical Society.*)

Stanton resigned her presidency, and Susan B. Anthony was elected to serve in her place.

Susan continued to petition Elizabeth for speeches at the suffrage conventions. Stanton spoke at many clubs, wrote articles for papers and magazines, and spent a good deal of time working on *The Woman's Bible*, the first volume of which was published in 1895 and the second volume in 1898. The book received strong criticism, especially from churches that labeled it blasphemous. Many newspapers in America and Europe carried the most unfavorable headlines and reviews that Elizabeth had ever seen before. But some newspapers, like the *New York Sun* and the *Chicago Post*, supported *The Woman's Bible*. One minister, the Reverend Alexander Kent of Washington, D.C., showed his support by commenting that it was not an attack on religion but an attack on false religious teachings about women. Susan B. Anthony also gave her support for the book.

Despite (or perhaps because of) the criticism, the book sold well. The first volume went through three American and two English editions. Though Elizabeth had been very clear that *The Woman's Bible* had nothing to do with the suffrage movement, the press and the public still linked the two. Many women within the suffrage movement did not like the book, nor did they like the fact that it was associated with their movement.

Elizabeth was not bothered by the criticism. In fact, she welcomed the heated discussion. She believed that at least it made people think. As always, that had been her primary objective.

In 1895, Elizabeth Cady Stanton turned eighty years old. Susan B. Anthony arranged to have the National Council of Women host her birthday celebration. Six thousand people attended the party at the Metropolitan Opera House, and thousands more sent letters and telegrams. Newspapers throughout America, even those opposed to women's suffrage, honored her with features and editorials. This outpouring of good feeling showed that although some of her ideas were not popularly accepted, she was still loved and greatly admired. One senator remarked, "Elizabeth has no enemies, merely friends who disagree with her."

In 1898, the fiftieth anniversary of the Seneca Falls Convention, Elizabeth published her autobiography, *Eighty Years and More, Reminiscences 1815-1897.* It reflected her personality—witty, lively, and insightful. It was a private look into many of the events she and Susan had written about in *History of Woman Suffrage.* Her autobiography was as widely praised as *The Woman's Bible* was criticized. By that time, she was considered a nationwide legend, the "Grand Old Woman," the elder stateswoman of the women's rights movement.

She continued to write constantly, although her eyesight was failing, and she maintained her active interest in politics and public affairs. She sent messages to the suffrage conventions to be read in her absence. On

October 12, 1902, she published a long article about divorce in the *New York American*. Elizabeth wrote in her diary that she was deeply touched by a postcard that she had received from an anonymous woman. It was to be Elizabeth's last entry in her diary, and she copied the woman's postcard, which read: "Today's *American* has a half-page that should be framed, or, better still, writ large or megaphoned everywhere. How many hearts today will thrill in response and how many heads will begin to think. It is by a Grand Old Woman. God bless her!"

On October 26, 1902, Elizabeth Cady Stanton died at three in the afternoon sitting quietly in her chair. She was almost eighty-seven years old. Just the day before, she had sent a letter to President Theodore Roosevelt, urging him to approve the Sixteenth Amendment enfranchising women, writing: "Abraham Lincoln immortalized himself by the emancipation of four million Southern slaves ... We now desire that you, Mr. President ... immortalize yourself by bringing about the complete emancipation of thirty-six million women."

All of her remaining children were present at her death. (Her eldest son, Daniel, had died in 1891.) Only family and a few close friends attended her funeral. In the weeks following, nearly every American newspaper honored her memory. Susan B. Anthony told one reporter:

For fifty years there has been an unbroken friend-

ship between us. We did not agree on every point
. . . We never listened to stories of each other,
never believed any tales of disloyalty of one to
the other. Mrs. Stanton was a most courageous
woman, a leader of thought and action. I have
always called her the statesman of our movement.

It took another eighteen years after Elizabeth's death
before the Nineteenth Amendment was ratified on August 20, 1920, granting women the right to vote. The
amendment would be dubbed the "Susan B. Anthony
Amendment" because Susan had remained solely fo-
cused on the issue of women's suffrage. The language of
the Nineteenth Amendment, however, remained the same
as when Elizabeth Cady Stanton had first written it as a
proposed Sixteenth Amendment in 1878.

Appendix

The Nineteenth Amendment
"The right of citizens of the United States to vote shall not be denied or abridged by the United States or by any State on account of sex."

A younger generation of activists continued the struggle of the American women's rights movement began by Elizabeth Cady Stanton and her contemporaries. Among them were Carrie Chapman Catt, founder of the League of Women Voters; Alice Paul, who would submit the first version of the Equal Rights Amendment to Congress in 1923; noted journalist Ida Bell Wells-Barnett; and Elizabeth Cady Stanton's daughter Harriot Eaton Stanton Blatch, who formed the Equality League of Self-Supporting Women, the first suffrage group that included working-class women.

These activists and others urged the passage of the Nineteenth Amendment which began its final legislative journey after World War I. In 1918, the amendment passed in the House of Representatives only to find defeat in the Senate. The Senate would debate for another year before approving women's suffrage, and finally by August 26, 1920, seventy-two years after the first women's rights convention in Seneca Falls, New York, enough states complied to ratify the amendment to the Constitution.

Timeline

1815—Born November 12 in Johnstown, New York.

1826—Eleazar Cady dies.

1830—Graduates from Johnstown Academy.

1831—Enters Troy Female Seminary.

1840—Marries Henry Brewster Stanton on May 1.
Attends first World Anti-Slavery Convention in London.

1842—Daniel Cady Stanton born.

1844—Henry Brewster Stanton, Jr. born.

1845—Gerrit Smith Stanton born.

1848—Organizes first women's rights convention in Seneca Falls, New York.

1851—Theodore Weld Stanton born.
Meets Susan Brownell Anthony.

1852—Margaret Livingston Stanton born.

1854—Becomes the first woman to address the New York State Legislature.

1856—Harriot Eaton Stanton born.

1859—Robert Livingston Stanton born.

1867—Travels to Kansas with Susan B. Anthony.

1868—Publishes the first issue of the *Revolution.*

1870—Sells the *Revolution.* Spends the next decade as a paid lecturer.

1880—Lucretia Mott dies.

1881—Publishes *History of Woman's Suffrage, Volume 1.*

1882—Publishes *History of Woman's Suffrage, Volume 2.*

1887—Henry Brewster Stanton dies.

1892—Delivers "The Solitude of Self."

1895—Publishes *The Woman's Bible.*

1898—Publishes autobiography, *Eighty Years and More: Reminiscences, 1815-1897.*

1902—Dies on October 26.

Bibliography

Barry, Kathleen. *Susan B. Anthony: A Biography*. New York: New York University Press, 1988.

Brill, Marlene Targ. *Let Women Vote!* Brookfield, CT: The Millbrook Press, 1996.

Bryant, Jennifer Fisher. *Lucretia Mott, A Guiding Light*. Grand Rapids, MI: William B. Eerdmans Publishing Company, 1996.

Cooper, Ilene. *Susan B. Anthony*. New York: Franklin Watts, An Impact Biography, 1984.

Dubois, Ellen Carol, Editor. *The Elizabeth Cady Stanton-Susan B. Anthony Reader: Correspondence, Writings, Speeches. Revised Editon*. Boston: Northeastern University Press, 1992.

Faber, Doris. *Oh Lizzie! The Life of Elizabeth Cady Stanton*. New York: Lothrop, Lee & Sheppard Company, 1972.

Flexner, Eleanor and Fitzpatrick, Ellen. *Century of Struggle, The Women's Rights Movement in the United States.* Cambridge, MA: The Belknap Press of Harvard University Press, 1996.

Fritz, Jean. *You Want Women to Vote, Lizzie Stanton?* New York: Penguin, 1995.

Griffith, Elisabeth. *In Her Own Right.* New York: Oxford University Press, 1984.

Gurko, Miriam. *The Birth of the Women's Rights Movement, The Ladies of Seneca Falls.* New York: Macmillan Publishing Co., Inc., 1974.

Harper, Judith. *Susan B. Anthony, A Biographical Companion.* Santa Barbara, CA: ABC-CLIO, Inc., 1998.

Kendell, Martha E. *Susan B. Anthony, Voice for Women's Voting Rights.* Springfield, NJ: Enslow Publishers, Inc., 1997.

Oakley, Ann B. *Elizabeth Cady Stanton.* Long Island, NY: The Feminist Press, 1972.

Schneir, Miriam. *Feminism: The Essential Historical Writings.* New York: Random House, 1972.

Stanton, Elizabeth Cady. *Eighty Years and More, Reminiscences 1815-1897.* Boston: Northeast University Press, 1993.

Stanton, Elizabeth Cady, Susan B. Anthony, and Matilda Joslyn Gage, editors. *History of Woman Suffrage, Volume 1, 1848-1861.* Salem, New Hampshire: Ayer Company, Publishers, Inc., Reprint Edition, 1985.

————. *History of Woman Suffrage, Volume 2, 1861-1876.* Salem, New Hampshire: Ayer Company, Publishers, Inc., Reprint Edition, 1985.

————. *History of Woman Suffrage, Volume 3, 1876-1885.* Salem, New Hampshire: Ayer Company, Publishers, Inc., Reprint Edition, 1985.

Suhl, Yuri. *Eloquent Crusader, Ernestine Rose.* New York: Julian Messner, 1970.

Sullivan, George. *The Day the Women Got the Vote, A Photo History of the Women's Rights Movement.* New York: Scholastic, 1994.

Ward, Geoffry. *Not For Ourselves Alone: The Story of Elizabeth Cady Stanton and Susan B. Anthony.* New York: Alfred A. Knopf, 1999.

Wheeler, Marjorie Spruill, Editor. *One Woman, One Vote, Rediscovering the Woman Suffrage Movement.* Troutdale, Oregon: NewSage Press, 1995.

Sources

CHAPTER ONE

p. 9, "Oh, my daughter . . ." Stanton, Elizabeth Cady. *Eighty Years and More, Reminiscences 1815-1897.* Boston: Northeastern University Press, 1993, p. 20.

p. 9, "I will try . . ." ibid., p. 21.

p. 10, "Hereafter let us . . ." ibid., p. 11.

p. 14, "throw himself on the grave . . ." ibid., p. 22.

p. 16, "Ah, you should have been . . ." Merriam, Eve. *Growing Up Female in America.* Garden City, New York: Doubleday & Company, Inc. 1971, p. 55.

p. 17, "When you are grown . . ." Oakley, Mary Ann B. *Elizabeth Cady Stanton.* Long Island, New York: The Feminist Press, 1972, p. 19.

p. 17, "Again, I felt . . ." Stanton, op.cit., 33-34.

p. 18, "Fear of judgment . . ." ibid., 43.

CHAPTER TWO

p. 23, "Dressed as a Quakeress . . ." Stanton, op.cit., 63.

p. 27, "Seek Truth for . . ." Bryant, Jennifer Fisher. *Lucretia Mott, A Guiding Light*. Grand Rapids, Michigan: William B. Eerdmans Publishing Company, 1996, p. 77.

p. 27, "If anyone can prove . . ." Oakley, op.cit., 33.

p. 28, "After battling so many . . ." ibid., p. 33.

CHAPTER THREE

p. 32, "The puzzling questions of . . ." Stanton, op. cit., pp. 112-13.

p. 34, "it is very remarkable . . ." Oakley, op. cit., p. 38.

p. 37, "The general discontent I felt . . ." Stanton, op. cit., p. 148.

CHAPTER FOUR

p. 38, "A convention to discuss . . ." Brill, Marlene Targ. *Let Women Vote!* Brookfield, Connecticut: The Millbrook Press, 1996, p. 26.

p. 40, "the power to make laws . . ." Oakley, op.cit., p. 46.

p. 42, "Most women . . ." Gurko, Mariam. *The Birth of the Women's Rights Movement, The Ladies of Seneca Falls*. New York: Macmillan Publishing Co., Inc., 1974, p. 100.

p. 44, "Insurrection Among Women!" Merriam, op. cit., p. 14.

p. 44, "The order of things . . ." Shul, Yuri. *Eloquent Crusader, Ernestine Rose*. New York: Julian Messner, 1970, p. 72.

CHAPTER FIVE
p. 49, "Laugh in your turn . . ." Oakley, op. cit., p. 49.

p. 54, "In thought and sympathy . . ." Kendall, Martha E. *Susan B. Anthony , Voice for Women's Voting Rights.* Springfield, New Jersey: Enslow Publishers, Inc., p. 68.

p. 56, "Let no drunkard be the father . . ." Oakley, op. cit., p. 56.

p. 58, ". . . a treasure, a friend and . . ." Merriam, op. cit., p. 65.

CHAPTER SIX
p. 60, "I learned it here . . ." Stanton, op. cit., pp. 188-89.

p. 61, "Let us say, in behalf of . . ." Oakley, op. cit., p. 61.

p. 61, ". . . You had the argument . . ." Stanton, op. cit., p. 199.

p. 62, "Ladies, it takes me no . . ." Oakley, op. cit., p. 62.

p. 63, "I passed through a terrible scourging . . ." Gurko, op.cit., p. 196.

p. 65, "Well, we claim our . . ." Suhi, op.cit., p. 141.

p. 66, "dried-up old maids . . ." Gurko, op.cit., p. 205.

CHAPTER SEVEN
p. 75, "We had a low, easy carriage . . ." Stanton, op.cit., p. 246.

p. 85, "I did not see . . ." Gurko, op. cit., p. 284.

CHAPTER EIGHT

p. 87, "the Bible was no more . . ." Oakley, op. cit., p. 130.

p. 88, "joy of deep soul-love," Griffith, Elisabeth. *In Her Own Right: The Life of Elizabeth Cady Stanton.* New York: Oxford University Press, 1984, p. 188.

p. 92, ". . . In discussing the sphere of man . . ." Oakley, op. cit., p. 126.

p. 96, "Today's *American* has a half-page . . ." ibid., p. 137.

p. 96, "Abraham Lincoln immortalized himself . . ." Gurko, op.cit., p. 300.

p. 96, "For fifty years there has been . . ." Oakley, op. cit., p. 138.

Index